More than an emotion, a fruit of the Spirit

joy

a devotional by

Vanessa Gracia Cruz

WestBow Press books may be ordered through booksellers or by contacting:

WestBow Press
A Division of Thomas Nelson & Zondervan
1663 Liberty Drive
Bloomington, IN 47403
www.westbowpress.com
1 (866) 928-1240

ISBN: 978-1-9736-6285-3 (sc)
ISBN: 978-1-9736-6287-7 (hc)
ISBN: 978-1-9736-6286-0 (e)

Library of Congress Control Number: 2019907095

Print information available on the last page.

WestBow Press rev. date: 6/10/2019

Dedicated to Levi, my miracle baby. I asked the Lord for you, and He heard my prayer, and out of my sadness came the greatest joy. You were so worth the wait.

Contents

Introduction

Last year, when the first edition of this book was released, I had still yet to see many of the promises I was believing for. No one knew at the time, but I began writing "Joy" in the wake of two miscarriages and two years of infertility. I was dealing with a few different conditions that made it not only hard for me to conceive, but uncomfortable to carry out my ministry because of the pain it caused, and side-effects of the medication I had to take.

I wrote this book at a time when I felt anything but joyful. I felt hopeless. In fact, not many people know, but I actually did not come out of that season of infertility and sickness until the book had already gone to print. Throughout the entire writing process, I felt the Lord prompting me to write in faith.

I would continuously question why He had put in my heart to write about joy in the midst of one of such a sad season. Wouldn't it have made more sense to put this topic on my heart while I was a joyful honeymooner or when my ministry was at a highpoint? I struggled while writing it and often wanted to give up. Sometimes out of anger, other times out of frustration, but mainly out of doubt. I would think: *surely, Lord I am being a hypocrite... What authority do I have to speak on joy right now?* But, time after time I would hear the Holy Spirit whisper: *I use broken things, and then I make them whole.* I kept writing because I had faith that God would restore my joy, and use my testimony to help others also be restored. It was while writing this book that I realized that pain doesn't disqualify from having joy. In fact, it is precisely what qualifies you.

What I did not know at the time the first edition was published was that two weeks after the final book was printed and we prepared to release it, I would learn I as pregnant with my son, Levi. In fact, as I write and revise for this second edition, my miracle is asleep in the room next to me. However, what was even more surprising than finally receiving what was promised, was that by the time I did, I no longer felt empty or hopeless. I had learned to cultivate joy in my heart even in the midst of loss and uncertainty. The Holy Spirit taught me how to change my heart without needing to change my circumstances; and I think that's the greatest lesson in this book.

The main message of this book is that you do not need everything in your life to be in order in order to live with joy. What you need is a relationship with the giver of joy: The Holy Spirit. If you don't learn that principle you will never have joy, even if you receive exactly what you've prayed for. You will be the mother who prayed for children but complains about their behavior; the wife who wishes for a husband, but disparages her marriage. Through this process, if there is anything I have learned it is that even when everything in your life is out of your control: having joy is within your grasp, because a relationship with God is within your grasp. And once you learn that, you will enjoy the journey to the promises God has for you.

I developed this devotional as a way for me myself to learn to cultivate joy after loss and sadness. I recognized that I needed a change in perspective more than I needed a change in my situation. I got that through spending time with Him and His word through daily study and meditations that I've written here for you. This book is meant to be read in pieces; one lesson at a time for fourteen days. I recommend that you find a quiet place, away from distractions, and read with an open heart. Set apart lots of time for you to meditate on the word, journal, and pour your heart out to God. The word "meditate" as used in the bible is translated literally as "to chew" or "to digest." I've discovered that the word of God is so much richer, and deeper, when I've turned it over and over in my mind and heart; when I mentally digest it throughout the day. Each lesson becomes clearer still when I process it by talking to God about it in prayer. Which is why at the end of each lesson, you'll find questions for meditation, and a prayer.

In this second edition of *Joy* I've revised some of the chapters, because now I have seen with my eyes what I used to only perceive in my Spirit: that while writing this book, even in my saddest season, I was on the verge of a breakthrough. Perhaps in this moment you find yourself in a time of grief or anxiety because of all the things in life you cannot control. Perhaps you have lost someone precious to you, or simply do not know where life is taking you. I pray that through this devotional the Holy Spirit gives you a new perspective on joy, and the ability to receive it, cultivate it, and live in it. Of course, this is by no means a complete theology. There are so many answers that you will need you seek in your time alone with God, that no one else can reveal to you. However, my prayer is that somehow, the words that the Lord spoke to me serve as a tool for you to learn how to produce joy in your heart, through time in the presence of its Creator, who loves you more than you know.

With Love,

Vanessa Garcia Cruz

1

The Fruit of Joy

*"But the fruit of the Spirit is love, **joy**, peace, patience, kindness, goodness, faithfulness, gentleness and self-control."*
Galatians 5:22-23 (NIV)

Often when we think of joy, we think of an emotion. We have been conditioned to think that joy is a response to something good that has happened, or the result of a favorable set of circumstances. Because we believe that joy is an emotion, we make the mistake of thinking it is out of our control. We assume that when things are going well (when God has answered all our prayers and we are celebrating our victories) joy will come automatically. We tend to believe the opposite is true as well- that if we are in the midst of pain or hardship, or if we are waiting for God to meet a need, that it is impossible to be joyful during that season.

This, my friends, is a lie of the enemy. He takes joy in convincing God's children that joy is dependent on circumstances. Sadly, he has managed to make many of us believe that joy out of our reach unless everything in our lives falls into place. He has deceived us into thinking that unless or until we get what we want we are resigned to a season of sadness, incompletion, or frustration.

Yet, through the verse above, we learn the true nature of joy, as designed by its creator. His word doesn't describe joy as an emotion, which could be fleeting, temporary, or fickle. In God's definition of joy, He describes it as a fruit. Like a fruit, it is something tangible, good for us, and most importantly can be *produced in us.* Just as you can produce fruit when there is none, and that fruit can nourish your physical body, the Holy Spirit can produce joy in your heart that can nourish your soul — even in the darkest of circumstances.

In God's definition of joy, He describes it as a fruit of the Spirit

The word of God reveals a simple truth that the enemy would never want us to know: that God, the creator of joy, did not place joy out of our reach or make its presence in our lives dependent on our circumstances. Instead, He benevolently created the nature of joy (as well as love, patience, goodness, and all the other fruits of the Spirit) to be a product of our relationship with Him. That is why you can see people living the most amazing seasons of their lives and still lack joy, while others experience the driest, most painful seasons and somehow remain joyful. The latter have learned how to grow the fruit of joy in their lives through the help of the Holy Spirit. They don't wait for their circumstances to change, telling themselves they will be happier when they get what they are waiting for, or that joy is unobtainable. They have learned to cultivate joy, and therefore enjoy its sweetness during every season of their lives.

The creator of joy, did not place joy out of our reach or make its presence in our lives dependent on our circumstances

Joy, like any other fruit, requires intentionality. No one ever stumbled upon a harvest. Any farmer or gardener can tell you that every fruit requires thoughtful planting, and must be intentionally produced. In the same way, we can not expect to accidentally stumble upon joy, or for it to blow in on the wind of the events in our lives. In order to reap it we have to make a conscious decision to do so. Just as a farmer works all year to ensure the health of his land, then carefully, diligently sows his seed; we too must ensure that we intentionally produce the fruits of the Spirit in our lives.

Firstly, in order for joy to grow in our hearts, we must evaluate the environment of our hearts. Just as earthly fruit requires healthy land to grow, we must have healthy hearts that will allow God to make something grow in them. The fruit of joy will never grow in a heart full of bitterness or malice. Neither can it thrive where there is lack of forgiveness or unwillingness to let the past go. If we want to have joy, we must be willing to bury our pasts, disillusions, and toxic emotions.

In Psalm 126:5 the same word that teaches us that joy is a fruit, teaches that our pain is the seed:

> *"Those who sow with tears will reap with songs of joy. Those who go out weeping, carrying seed to sow, will return with songs of joy..."*
> *Psalm 126:5-6 (NIV)*

One of the greatest lessons I have learned in my life is that in God's eyes pain is never the final product. Pain is meant to be the seed that we sow. God's intention is to cause it to blossom into joy at the right time. As we let go of our past, and our despair, we make room for a harvest of joy. Often the reason why we see no growth of joy in our hearts is because we are unwilling to let go of the seed that is our pain. We harbor our pain and sadness and cling to our depression. The first step in a journey towards joy is giving those things to the Lord and allowing them to die in order to bring new life. Look at how it is described in the book of John:

I have learned in my life is that pain, in God's eyes, is not the final product

"Truly, truly, I tell you, unless a kernel of wheat falls to the ground and dies, it remains only a seed; but if it dies, it bears much fruit."
John 12:24 (Berean Study Bible)

As you read these words, think about what you are doing to work towards producing joy in your life. Have you been waiting for circumstances to bring you joy? Have you been unwilling to let go of things that cause you pain? Consider what the word says of the virtuous woman:

"...out of her earnings she plants a vineyard. She sets about her work vigorously; her arms are strong for her tasks."
Proverbs 31:15-17 (NLT)

Although this scripture isn't referring specifically to joy, it teaches us that a wise woman leaves nothing to chance. She is fierce and strong, and rises early to make sure her needs are met. In the same way, we are each responsible for vigorously working towards planting a vineyard of joy in our own hearts. We cannot expect this task to fall to anyone else, and we cannot expect it to happen by simply wishing for it.

Many of us have allowed ourselves to become victims of the circumstances in our lives. We have believed the enemy's lie that joy is for some but not for others. But if this were true, God would be an unfair God; and we know that He is not. The *truth* is that we all have the choice to allow the Holy Spirit to grow joy in us. This takes time, and it requires us to be active rather than passive. In his first letter to the Corinthians, Paul wrote, "I planted the seed, another watered it, **but God has made it grow**." In the same way, there will be many times in our lives when we will need to prepare the soil, and plant the seed, so that God can grow the fruit of joy in us.

The Spirit is water that brings growth to our joy and makes it possible.

Today I ask you: are you willing to rise early, and work passionately to provide for your spiritual need of joy? Many of us have been hungry for joy. So much so that we feel we cannot go on, or won't make it another day, but still haven't done our part to ensure that fruit is produced in us. The wise woman, however, plants an entire vineyard of what she needs, so that she will never hunger again. Have you ever considered planting a vineyard of joy for yourself? Not waiting for it to fall into your lap, but actually taking steps to develop a relationship with God that will give fruit?

Thoughts for Meditation:

Have I considered joy to be out of my reach? Do I believe joy is available for me if I want it?

What does this tell me about my view of God and His character?

Have I been waiting for joy to come to me without doing my part to cultivate it?

What can I do to cultivate joy in my life? What seeds can I plant?

What weeds need to be pulled out so that my heart can become fertile soil? Are there roots of bitterness, jealousy, or anger keeping me from obtaining joy?

Prayer: 

Holy Spirit, I believe that you are the producer of joy, and I long for you to make my heart fruitful ground. So that I may have joy to nourish my soul, and be used to bring joy to others. Make me able to plant a vineyard of joy in my heart. Teach me to do my part, and to plant seeds of joy, and bring growth as you water them with your Spirit. Uproot anything that hinders the growth of my harvest. For joy is your promise to me, and from this day on, I receive it.

2

Where Joy is Made

"You make known to me the path of life; in your presence there is fullness of joy; at your right hand are pleasures forevermore."
Psalm 16:11(NIV)

Some would say I was born with a bible in my hand. I grew up in church. My parents were pastors, and taught my siblings and I about God from the very beginning of our lives. So, I grew up with knowledge of certain truths. The verse above, for example, I knew by heart. Whether it was because of the songs we sung in church, or memorizing the word in Sunday School, I knew that there was *supposed* to be joy in the presence of God. I knew these things as sweet and pleasant words, but not much more.

It's easy to read a verse or sing a worship song and forget that the words in them are meant to be more than decoration in our cluttered lives. The fact that joy is found in the presence of God, is not just a nice sentiment, it is truth. And the word says that truth has the power to set us free. We need only to learn to use that power, and live in truth. Too many of us remain bound by anxiety or fear because

> *Many of us however, remain in bondage, because we don't live by the truth*

we have overlooked the fact that joy is readily available to us. We want it, but we have forgotten where to look.

Like many others, I *knew* that joy was supposed to come from God. I was *supposed* to be living life in abundance— hadn't that been what I was taught my whole life? Yet, I suffered with depression and anxiety for years. I remember being in the sixth grade, and calling my mom from the bathroom, begging her to come pick me up because I could not stop crying. I was too young to know that I was experiencing a panic attack. I remember going through my teens struggling with loneliness and depression even though I knew of God, believed in Him and loved Him.

I lived shackled in a loop of depression and anxiety because I didn't ever go to the place where joy is made

The problem was, the *presence* of God wasn't a place I went very often. Although I believed in God, I didn't spend any time with Him. I had a religion, and a title, but not a relationship with God. I lived shackled to depression and anxiety because I didn't ever go to the place where joy is made; the place where there was power to set me free.

It wasn't until I began to seek the presence of God that things began to change in my life. I finally realized that the title of "Christian" is not enough to heal your heart or get you through difficult circumstances. In fact, the title does nothing at all. If you want to see changes in your life- if you want to be healed, be free, and have joy- you'll need to actually spend time in the presence of God.

Religion doesn't bring joy

Religion doesn't bring joy. In fact, since the beginning of the word of God, He's been telling His people that what is in our hearts has always been infinitely more important than religious routine. To be clear, I'm not saying that we shouldn't obey the teachings of our faith. Only that if we do those things and our hearts remain far from God, they are of little value. Look at what the Lord says to His people:

> *"I desire steadfast love and not sacrifice, the knowledge of God rather than burnt offerings." Hosea 6:6 (ESV)*

Steadfast love–that's what matters to God. That's what makes the difference in our lives. The word steadfast means unchanging and consistent. When we learn the importance of honest, consistent, unchanging love for God, we begin to experience more than just religion. We begin to experience relationship. In Hosea 6:6 it also says He desires for us to have "*knowledge of God*" – He wants us to know Him. He wants us to learn about Him as we would a friend or a loved one with whom we've spent time.

> *When we learn the importance of honest, consistent, unchanging love for God, we begin to experience more than just religion, but relationship*

How do we get to that place? When we to talk to Him and spend time with Him. It's in our private devotional time. Look what happens during this time according to the psalm we are focusing on today:

> *"You make known to me the path of life; in your presence there is fullness of joy"*

Relationship with God brings knowledge of the path of life. The more time we spend with Him the less confused and worried we will be; the more confident we will be in our decisions. We will have more insight we will have on the situations occurring around us. Only He knows what's next, and what is best for us. But He shares these things with us when we go to Him and spend time in prayer and meditation on His word.

Equally important, relationship with God brings joy. So many of us pray for joy but refuse to go to the source: the presence of God. Many of us spend years seeing small flashes of joy in fleeting moments, but find that it disappears just as quickly as it came. In our last chapter we learned that joy is a fruit: it is the product of the Holy Spirit. We also learned that fruit is always produced intentionally. If we don't intentionally spend time in his presence, we will never experience fullness of joy.

So many of us pray for joy but refuse to go to the source: the presence of God

In reality, it's not our condition that needs to change, but our position.

Fullness means complete, whole, and lacking nothing. It means that when we learn to seek the kind of joy that is found in nearness to God, we begin to experience full joy, not just fleeting happiness. There are so many people, even Christians who do not know this kind of joy even though it is available to them. That was my case for many years. Laziness, busyness, and distraction kept me from finding fullness of joy until I decided to intentionally spend time with God on a daily basis. Not because of rules, religion, or being afraid of punishment. Because I discovered that it gave me the happiness I desired but had been missing for so long.

I heard this saying once: "joy is not the absence of trouble, but the presence of God." We often think that conditions need to be perfect in order for us to feel joy. In reality, it's not our condition that needs to change, but our **position**. When we are far from God, we will experience lives that lack all the things God brings (as we read in the last chapter: love, joy, peace, etc.) But as we draw near to God, we reap the rewards of being in His presence. The word of God says:

> *"...whoever would draw near to God must believe that he exists and that he rewards those who [diligently] seek him."*
> *Hebrews 11:6 (ESV)*

Those who draw near to God must be more than just "card-carrying" Christians. It takes more than a church membership. We are rewarded when we diligently seek Him (New King James Version). Here we see another reference to being steadfast, consistent and unchanging, as described in Hosea 6.

I want to challenge you to spend time in God's presence as you read this book. My prayer is that you would go beyond the title of Christian, and become one who diligently seeks God and reaps the benefits of His presence. Reading books and watching sermons are great. But if in the end you don't learn to diligently seek God on your own, you will never receive lasting joy.

As you go through this devotional, take time to pray, journal, and meditate in the presence of God. Find a quiet place to talk with God and pour out your heart to Him. It is in these moments where joy is made, and your heart will be renewed day by day.

Thoughts for Meditation:

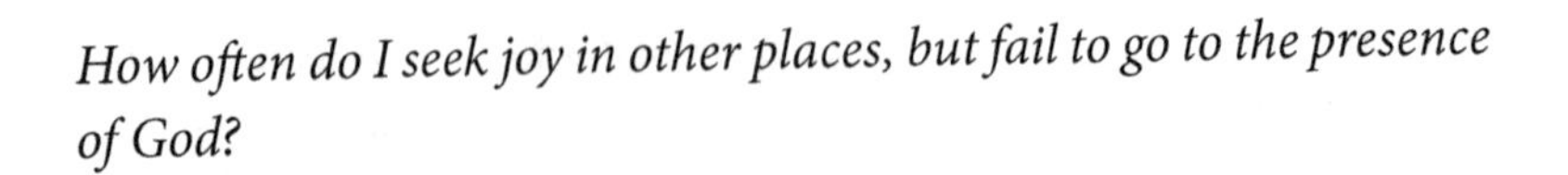

How often do I seek joy in other places, but fail to go to the presence of God?

Have I been steadfast and diligent in my devotion to the Lord?

Over the next 14 days as I read this book, how can I ensure that I make time to find joy in His presence?

Prayer:

Lord, teach me how to find fullness of joy in your presence. I'm sorry if I've offered you religion, but have never offered steadfast love and devotion. I'm sorry if I have never gotten to know you. I realize now that I am in need of a relationship with you. Teach me how to seek you in a way that is consistent and diligent so that I can reap the rewards of knowing you. Make known to me the paths of life, and show me who you are, so that I can experience the joy only you can give.

3

Joy Conquers Anxiety

"Do not be anxious about anything, but in every situation, by prayer and petition, with thanksgiving, present your requests to God."
Philippians 4:6 (NIV)

One of the reasons joy is so difficult to obtain is because we live in a stress-saturated world. Our culture demands that we be efficient and fast paced. Our own expectations drive us to be perfectionists and control-oriented. Even our family and friends demand that we be the perfect balance of loyal yet un-clingy. We strive to reach perfection. We want to be everything for everyone, all the time. And, you know what? *That's okay.* It's okay to want to be balanced, successful, and well-liked. What isn't okay is thinking we can do so all on our own.

God never meant for you to reach success using only your own ability. He knew you wouldn't have time for it all and that you would slip up and need help along the way. In fact, when we really think about it, much of our anxiety stems from being unsure if we have enough strength to conquer in the face of challenges. We subconsciously know

God never meant for you to reach success using only your own ability

that we don't, so our brains go into over-drive producing alerts. Our body produces hormones to warn us that the situation we are facing is too difficult for us. That is where stress comes from, and it's one of joy's strongest and most unrelenting rivals. In a single swoop it can cause health issues, unhappiness, and fear, that in turn only cause more and more stress. It's a virus that picks at our joy, making it impossible to keep.

That is where stress comes from, and it's one of joy's strongest and most successful rivals

But I love Philippians 4:6 because, to me it simplifies stress. It reassures what our hearts already know deep down: **we need God's help**. We need His protection and guidance in order to conquer the pain that life brings. And the great news is that if we are in a season where we are anxious, or unsure, we can take it to Him and let Him sort it out. I consider this a win-win. After all, I can't handle the unknown and I really don't know what's best for my life anyway. Why not, then, just hand it over to the one person who does: God?

This verse tells us we don't need to make sense out of the mess we may find ourselves in, we don't have to be perfect, or find a way to make sure everything turns out ok- that's God's job. All we have to do is let Him know what we're going through and be grateful in advance that He'll hear us and supply our need. The way I see it, this verse is saying: change your point of view. Stop seeing things that happen in your life as obstacles. That viewpoint produces fear and anxiety. Start seeing them as requests that you can present to God as you ask him to be a part of your solution. And because everything the Bible says about God points to the fact that he *wants* to be a part of your life, you can trust Him to help in your time of need.

You have the choice whether or not you are going to be anxious. If you didn't, the word of God wouldn't command it: "*do not be anxious about anything.*" Honestly, I am just as guilty as anyone else of thinking, *"what do you mean? I can't help it if I worry."* But I can, and so can you. The verse at hand does not say "try not to worry" it tells us simply not to do it. Which means it is possible to quit anxiety. Stress is the result of dozens of anxious thoughts about things you can't control but are unwilling to lay at God's feet. Joy, however, is the result of training your mind to take things to Him instead.

You have the choice whether or not you are going to be anxious

When I first began to study this verse, I memorized it. Anytime I received bad news, or experienced a setback I would repeat to myself, *"DO NOT BE ANXIOUS!"* In those moments, I instantly said a silent prayer about whatever was bothering me.

"In every situation, by prayer and petition, present your requests to God..."

This became a habit that I still continue today. I used to tense up, and remain so tense throughout the day that I'd get a headache. When my mom passed away, I became so anxious about my life, so convinced that bad things would happen, that I got jitters every time the phone would ring. But living that way made it impossible to be joyful. I had to learn to trust God, and pray instead of worry.

This doesn't mean I never feel worried or afraid about anything in my life. That would make me superhuman. It simply means I make the choice not to allow it to grow into panic or anxiety. It's a decision. I *decided* that there is nothing in the world that I should give enough power over me to make me anxious. There is no point; if I've already presented my request to God, He will be the one to work it out.

I decided that there is nothing in the world that I should give enough power over me to make me anxious

If anything bad is going to happen I trust that in the end, it'll work together for my good (see Romans 8:28). Because I have that confidence, I can present my requests to God with a thankful heart. There is so much joy in knowing that I don't have to be sure that everything is going to go according to plan. I just have to do the best I can on my end and trust that things always go according to God's plan.

If you struggle with stress or anxiety, I encourage you to memorize this verse the way I did. I wrote it out on a post-it and carried it everywhere I went. I made it a habit to pray instead of worry. In a very short time I began to feel more joy each day. If only our culture knew that there is a God who loves us, who doesn't want us to be destroyed and tortured by stress. He is willing to help us in our every need!

Thoughts for Meditation:

What is going on in your life right now that is out of your control? What are the thoughts that come up that trigger anxiety in your day to day?

List some things that you often try to do in your own strength, and forget to take to God and ask for help:

How could you present those things as petitions to God? What could you take off your worry-list, and trust Him to sort out?

Take some time to give thanks in advance for what you believe God could do in your life. Make a praise list for things he has already done!

Prayer:

Lord, I make the decision today to stop being anxious. Instead, in everything, I will bring ***you*** *my requests. I will trust that you know what is best for me, and that you will never let me down. Give me the strength to resist the temptation to stress when I don't know how things are going to work out. Holy Spirit, when things get rough, remind me to pray, so that difficult situations bring me closer to you, instead of further away.*

4

He Will Not Abandon Me

"Therefore my heart is glad and my tongue rejoices; my body also will rest in hope, because you will not abandon me to the realm of the dead, you will not let your holy one see decay. You have made known to me the paths of life; you will fill me with joy in your presence."
Acts 2:26-28 (NIV)

When I look back at the most difficult moments in my life, I only vaguely remember the details of those times. Most of the details are blurred in my memory. I can't remember anything else about those days, I just walked around in shock, in a fog. I remember the painful days after I had suffered through miscarriages.. It felt as though I was wasting away in sleepless nights and days with no appetite. As the stress increased, my concern for myself and my health diminished, and my body weakened. Even when I closed my eyes to rest, there was no rest to be found. Only replays of my fears on the big screen of my mind.

Even when I closed my eyes to rest, there was no rest to be found

It was during these times where I began to understand what it is like to feel as though you are living in the realm of the dead; as though you are trapped in a land where nothing can live or grow, and there is only loss. Maybe, dear friend, this is where you find yourself now. Maybe you are in a darkness so thick you can't see through the haze. Maybe you are stuck in what can only be described as the land of the dead. I've been there and I know the pain, the fear, and the disappointment. However, I also know that God never abandons us there. We can rest confidently in hope, because our God doesn't forget about us.

"my body also will rest in hope, because you will not abandon me to the realm of the dead"

If you look for the passage above in the bible, you will find it in two different places. The psalmist wrote them originally, but the words were prophetic and described how Jesus felt when he was crucified.

King David spoke of the land of the dead as he described overcoming deep emotional despair. Jesus had to actually descend to the land of the dead (into hell) after he was crucified in order to conquer death for us. The situations were similar: both had to brave what looked like ultimate defeat, yet neither was abandoned by their Heavenly Father.

Ultimately, they both conquered the place that threatened to defeat them, and were filled with the joy of the presence of God. Our takeaway is this: **the realm of the dead is not our final destination.** It is a passageway through to His presence, where there is fullness of joy. He will not leave you in your pain forever. His intention is to restore you and uplift you.

The realm of the dead is not our final destination

"you will not let your holy one see decay"

What more, He will not allow you to decay in the process. Have you ever questioned whether you will be left in one piece after a storm in your life? Sometimes it can seem as though the battle has deteriorated us, and worn us down. The word decay means to decline in excellence, health or prosperity. Decay occurs when we gradually become less of who God made us to be, and more of what the realm of the dead has gotten us used to. Little by little, many who have experienced heartache find that they don't smile like they used to, or can't trust anymore. Their bodies are exhausted, and their spirit is crushed. They experience a sad truth that is described in Proverbs: "*A joyful heart is good medicine, but a crushed spirit dries up the bones.*" *(Proverbs 17:22 NIV).*

"You have made known to me the paths of life;
you will fill me with joy in your presence."

God reassures us that he makes known to us the paths of life when we have lost our way. As we draw near to his presence, His kindness and mercy restore us, so that we are no longer decayed and deteriorated. Only His presence can restore what was once lost and make us whole again. And it is in this nearness to God, this return to his presence that he fills us with joy.

A few years ago I was at a youth retreat with the young people of our church. During one of the breaks, a young girl of about 17 years of age approached me with a downcast face. We had been ministering that day about letting go, forgiving, and allowing God to heal our wounds.

As we draw near to his presence, His kindness and mercy restore us, so that we are no longer decayed and deteriorated

She said to me, "Vanessa, I just don't know if I can let go." I asked her why she felt this way and she replied, "I feel as though if I let go of my pain, I will be empty. So much of me is tied into what happened to me as a child, without it, I don't know who I am." Just then, I felt the Holy Spirit nudge me to reassure her.

We were sitting beneath the shade of a huge, healthy tree that spread out in all directions. I said to her, "Do you see this tree? If it were to be uprooted, there would be a huge gaping hole, right?" "Right," she replied.

So I continued: "But if the owners of this land love what belongs to them, they would never leave leave a big gaping hole in the center of it. Rather, if this tree were to ever be uprooted, I'm sure they would plant another, just as big and beautiful in its place. In the same way, when God uproots the hurt in our lives, He doesn't leave us empty, He fills us with His presence."

That young girl was so afraid that she would deteriorate. She was worried that her decay had done so much damage, that letting go of her past would leave a hole in her heart. But fortunately for her, and for us, Jesus fills that hole with joy. In many cases, He restores us to such an extent that we have double what we had before:

"Instead of your shame there shall be a double portion; instead of dishonor they shall rejoice in their lot; therefore, in their land they shall possess a double portion; they shall have everlasting joy."
Isaiah 61:7 (NIV)

If today you find yourself feeling lost in a season of death and sorrow, know that God does not intend to leave you there. As I said in the first chapter of this book, your pain is not your final destination, but a bridge to a double portion of joy.

Thoughts for Meditation:

Where do I find myself at this moment in my life? Do I feel as though I am in the realm of the dead?

Do my soul and spirit need to rest in hope? Am I tired of the battle I have been fighting?

What kind of decay have I seen in my heart? How can I ask God to restore to me the joy of His presence?

Prayer:

Dear Lord, I thank you because I know you will never abandon me to the realm of the dead. Instead, you protect me from decay and total deterioration. Restore me, Lord. Bring me life, again. Fill me with the joy of your presence. Make known to me the paths of life.

5

I Will Not Be Shaken

"Cast your burden on the Lord, and he will sustain you;
He will never let the righteous to be shaken."
Psalm 55:22 (NIV)

Sometimes, the hardest part of going through trials isn't even the trial we are going through. It's the fear that the situation you are facing is going to rob you of the good in your life; or as this verse says, cause you to be shaken. We often fear that we are one mistake, one misstep away from being having to start over, removing the blessings we've received and the things we are proud to have built. Sometimes, we believe this to such an extent, that we sabotage ourselves by giving up or not doing our best because we are so afraid to fail. But God's word gives us two promises, through Psalm 55:22. If we can learn to believe and live by these promises, we will be much more likely to maintain an attitude of joy when we feel we are in danger of being shaken.

The first promise is that He will sustain us. The word "sustain" according to Webster's has two definitions: the first, is "to provide what is needed for someone to continue." When the word of God tells us that He will sustain us, it means that he is going to take on the responsibility of making sure we have everything we need to go the distance. It means that when the road gets tough and it feels like we can't go on, He is going to provide whatever it is that we lack to make sure we don't give up.

The second definition of the word 'sustain' is "to hold up the weight of something." If you notice, the verse we are studying starts out with a reference to something heavy: our burdens (all of our worries, fears, and inadequacies) and it tells us to cast them on the Lord because he will "sustain" (hold up the weight). The promise is this: we don't have to be nervous about failing, because if anything is ever too heavy, He will hold up the weight for us. If we stop to reflect on the significance of this, and let it sink into our hearts, there's truly nothing that should ever scare us or make us feel like we will not succeed. Neither stress nor fear are necessary because our burdens don't have to be sustained by our own strength but simply given over to God, who is more than able to sustain them.

He is going to provide whatever it is that we lack to make sure we don't give up

The next promise in this verse is that the Lord will "*never let the righteous to be shaken.*" In another version, it says he will "*never permit the righteous to be moved.*" That fear that we all have of being displaced isn't as realistic as the enemy would like us to think. God has given us His word that He will not allow anyone or anything to move us from where we are supposed to be. Through Jesus, we have been made righteous (*2 Corinthians 5:21*), and through our relationship with God we are given confidence that this word is ours to keep and to believe. We will not be knocked around, shaken, or moved. The things that we work hard for, that God has allowed us to build, are ours to keep, if only we remember to cast our burdens on the Lord.

That fear that we all have of being displaced isn't as realistic as the enemy would like us to think

Thoughts for Meditation:

Are you weary or burdened? Take some time to write why…

Reflect on how you feel after making a sincere effort to give God your burdens, what changes?

What are ways you can make casting your burdens on Him a more frequent habit?

Prayer:

Lord, there are times when I feel so weary and weighed down. I need you to help me, and give me rest for my soul. I'm tired of trying to carry all of my burdens on my own. I'm willing to lay them on you and trust that you will take them from me.

6

The Worries of This Life

"...But the worries of this life, the deceitfulness of wealth and the desires for other things come in and choke the word, making it unfruitful."Mark 4:19 (NIV)

By now, we have learned that joy is more than an emotion. It is a fruit produced from time in God's presence. And, we've begun to see a trend in verses that teach us how to seek joy in our lives: it's purposeful and intentional. Yet, here, the word points to something that can make our efforts to produce joy sterile and unfruitful: worry.

The level to which we allow worry to interfere with our joy is within our control

To some degree, it's understandable; worry is a natural reaction to challenges. We worry when we have disagreements with the people we love or when we want to do well at something new. We worry when things don't go our way and when we are forced to grow and change. There is no way to completely prevent worrisome situations. However, the level to which we allow worry to interfere with our joy *is* within our control.

In Mark 4:19, the Bible describes worry as one of the things that can choke the word of God in your life— killing the joy, faith, and peace that it produces— making it unfruitful. The worries of this world cause our heart to be divided and confused. Think of the things mentioned in this verse and how they affect our hearts and minds:

For one, the deceitfulness of wealth. We lose so much joy when we worry about money and are driven by greed. The illusion is that money and material possessions will make us happy, when in reality only God can fill the void in our hearts. So often we worry about not having the things we want and how those things are going to make us look in front of the people around us. But wealth, as stated in this verse, is deceitful. The only thing we achieve by worrying about it, is to choke the word of God that actually has the power to prosper us.

In this verse, Jesus also mentions desires for other things. Here, I believe He is referring to the constant desire we have for things other than the presence of God. The bible teaches us that in His presence there is fullness of joy. This means our joy is complete and lacking nothing as we draw nearer to our creator. The world tells us that we will be satisfied when we look better, have more friends, and make all of our problems go away. So, we mistakenly hope that a relationship, a career, a pill or a bottle can make us happy. We do not realize these things do not produce fullness of joy. They can make us happy temporarily, but ultimately they will leave us wanting.

This means our joy is complete and lacking nothing as we draw nearer to our creator

Psalm 103:5 tells us that God "*satisfies our desires with good things*" (NIV) and that when he does so our youth is renewed. He has the power to satisfy us with things that are good rather than harmful. Lasting, rather than temporary.

We don't need to chase these things because they are supplied by simply coming to Him. In Him, we find freedom from the worries of this world. Our job is to learn to seek Him before we begin to worry about wealth and all the other things that rob us of our peace. When we do this, He fills us with joy and renews our "youth"— our strength, our vigor, and our energy.

Thoughts for Meditation:

Have you ever tried reading the word of God, but found it unable to produce change in your life? Why do you think this was?

Have you ever let worry keep the word from giving fruit in your life?

Even now, are you struggling to chase after wealth or the things of this world?

Read Mark 4 and meditate on what Jesus is trying to teach his disciples about His word.

Prayer:

Heavenly Father, help me when the worries of this world threaten to choke the joy my life. Keep my heart from being divided. Protect me from desires for things that will not satisfy me, and help me to desire you, above all things. For you alone can satisfy my soul, and give me joy.

7

Grief Turns to Joy

"Very truly I tell you, you will weep and mourn while the world rejoices. You will grieve, but your grief will turn to joy. A woman giving birth to a child has pain because her time has come; but when her baby is born she forgets the anguish because of her joy that a child is born into the world. So with you: Now is your time of grief, but I will see you again and you will rejoice, and no one will take away your joy."
John 16:20-24 (NIV)

It's hard to conceive what the disciples were feeling when Jesus said these words to them. Their friend, their leader, their protector was no longer going to be physically with them, but instead was going to be publicly crucified and then taken away from this earth. I can only imagine the fear they must have felt. As disciples of Jesus they would be persecuted, and would no longer have their savior tangibly with them for guidance or comfort.

I imagine their confusion, as they questioned why, He, the bread of life would have to endure such a painful death, when all he had done was please the Father. And most vividly, I imagine their pure grief, as they prepared to mourn their friend. I bet they asked themselves: *Why is He leaving us? What are we going to do without Him?*

Jesus, of course, saw what his disciples were going through. Although I am sure that He himself was saddened by the fact that in a short time He was to be crucified, our loving, compassionate Savior made sure to comfort his friends. He essentially says to them: "My friends, I know you are sad. In fact, you are now in a time of grief, BUT this grief will not last forever."

Isn't it amazing that Jesus does not deny our pain?

Isn't it amazing that Jesus does not deny our pain? He acknowledges and understands when we grieve. He didn't turn to his disciples in anger that they were making things all about them, or lecture them about how they were questioning God.

He didn't, like many religious people tend to do, chastise them for their lack of faith, as if grief were a sin, or a crime against God. He didn't diminish their pain by saying something like "You think you have it rough? Try having to die on a cross!" No. Instead, Jesus comforted them.

In fact, the first message He gave to his disciples as he saw their hurt was this: It's okay to grieve. Jesus understood that they would have to go through a process of grief. They would need to process the loss of their savior. They would need to go through a time where the whole world would rejoice, while they were in sadness. How many times have we found ourselves in a painful situation and wondered if anyone cared what we were going through? How many times have we gone to friends in search of comfort only to be made feel as though our situation were insignificant? Jesus understood. He said to them, "now is your time of grief." In other words, "I understand that this hurts." Perhaps for someone reading this, now is a time of grief. Maybe all the people around you have failed to recognize the depth or the importance of what happened to you. Maybe they diminish it or make it seem meaningless.

A joy is coming that no one will be able to take away

If that is the case, I hope you feel the sweet

words of Jesus as He says to you that a joy is coming that no one will be able to take away.

You see, Jesus' acceptance of our grief is only the first step of how he heals and comforts us. He recognizes it, but He does not intend for us to grieve forever. The next part is even more powerful. It is when He assures us that our grieving makes way for beautiful, lasting joy. Because what Jesus' disciples didn't know up until that point is that although He would have to die, and both He and they would have to endure the heartache of the cross, that heartache was precisely what would open up a door for them to be able to go directly to The Father. And even more amazing, once they had access to The Father, nothing would be impossible for them! The doors would be open to anything they ask, and their joy would be *complete*. The more I learn about Jesus, the more I am convinced that His intention is for our joy to be complete.

Our grieving makes way for beautiful, lasting joy

All He desires is for us to live a life that is abundant and whole. But that doesn't mean that times of grief would not still be a part of life.

He compares it to the process of a woman giving birth. When I published the first edition of *Joy* I had not yet experienced this. However now, I can speak with authority on the matter. Giving birth to my son was absolutely the most painful thing I have ever done. The pain was intense, and grueling, and in many cases even dangerous. But after all, it is temporary, and the bundle of joy you take home afterwards is permanent, and no one can take it away from you. In the same way, we will grieve many times in our lives. We were never promised a perfect existence. However, the promise we *were* given is that there is always a blessing at the end of the time of grief; and that once we have received it, it is ours to keep, to love, and to enjoy.

Thoughts for Meditation:

Have I taken my grief to the Lord? Have I allowed myself to be open and vulnerable with my sadness in His presence?

Have I doubted that my sadness is important to Jesus? Have I felt that I would be judged, quieted, or turned away?

Have I ever considered that my pain could be bringing forward great joy?

Prayer:

Today, in your own words take some time to talk to Jesus about your time of grief. Lay every burden and worry at His feet, and allow Him to comfort you. Psalm 34:8 says the Lord is near to the broken hearted. As you go to Him now, ask for His presence to be near you as you receive healing for your heart.

8

That Your Joy May Be Complete

"Very truly I tell you, my Father will give you whatever you ask in my name. Until now you have not asked for anything in my name. Ask and you will receive, and your joy will be complete."
John 16:20-24 (NIV)

Originally there was only supposed to be one chapter in this book based on John 16. But as I wrote, a certain phrase in the passage continued to echo in my spirit, and began to minister to my heart: "*until now, you have not asked anything in my name.*" It is so subtly sandwiched between such powerful verses about joy and grief that one could read this passage hundreds of times and fail to see the importance of what Jesus is saying here.

"Until now, you have not asked anything in my name"

He is saying that for a long time, not even his own disciples had the power, the privilege, or the wisdom to pray the correct way. Yes, they knew Jesus. They were his closest followers and friends. No one knew him as much as they. They saw his power, believed in Him, and were loved by him. But they had never prayed the kind of prayer that moved mountains. Up until then, they had never asked for anything in *His name,* and because of that, their joy was incomplete.

The word "*complete*" in this passage is the Hebrew word "*pleroo*" which is used to describe something that has been poured out until overflowing, as well as something that is *fulfilled*. It is the feeling one gets when the desires of the heart have been accomplished. When you finally see something you have prayed for physically, before you. Manifested. Substantiated. It is essentially a dream (or a prayer) come true. What Jesus is saying here, is that when we ask for things in His name, we will receive the satisfaction that comes from seeing our prayers realized. Wouldn't we all be joyful if we knew that we would actually receive what we've asked for?

Wouldn't we all be joyful if we knew that we would actually receive what we've asked for?

Is there any greater joy than asking the Lord for something and knowing that He's heard, and that He will answer? As I studied this, I had to ask: *So then, Lord, why is it that so few people ever experience this joy?* He answered:

"until now, [they] have not asked anything in my name"

Now, I began to understand. I realized how many times we want things, even *need* things, but do not ask in Jesus' name. We often question why we do not receive the desires of our hearts. Why so much time passes between the onset of our needs, and their fulfillment. I wonder how many times the answer to our inquiry is that we simply haven't asked, or haven't asked the right way.

If we want to receive answers to our prayers, and the joy that comes with them, first of all we need to ask God for them. Of course, that sounds like common sense, yet, if there is anything I've learned from my time as a pastor it's how often we use prayer as a last resort, instead of a first response. When we are in need, our tendency is to try to solve our problem by physical means.

We try to think it out, solve it ourselves, or even bring it to family and friends. We often neglect to pray about it until it's already gotten out of hand. Even then, when we pray about it, we sometimes vent, cry, even question God, but forget to simply ask for His help. Maybe it's because we are afraid He won't answer.

Maybe it's because we believe that if we ask, God will see us as selfish or resent us for asking, but that is simply not true. In fact, there are many places in the Bible where our Heavenly Father encourages us to ask. He exhorts us to ask for our needs, for joy, and even for the gift of the Holy Spirit. As we read in Philippians 4:6, *"Be anxious for nothing, but in everything by prayer and supplication with thanksgiving let your requests be made known to God. (NIV)* This shows us that it's ok to make requests of God. He wants to hear them. Jesus also teaches us:

"If you, then, though you are evil, know how to give good gifts to your children, how much more will your Father in heaven give good gifts to those who ask him!"
Mathew 7:11 (NIV)

So you see, we need to ask. We need to begin to pray before we are in crisis; before our back is up against the wall. In the moment that we need Him, we can call on Him and trust that He will answer.

Then, we need to make sure we are asking in Jesus' name. I remember when I was my father's administrative assistant, during the year I worked towards my Master's degree. One of the key parts of my job was walking around our offices giving assignments, then checking back and making sure they were completed. Once, someone asked me if I ever felt shy or embarrassed about telling so many people what to do or if I ever wondered whether the people were going to comply. My reply was simple: "I don't

We need to begin to pray before we are in crisis

have to feel uncomfortable, because they know that when I ask something it's not for me, but what my father wants." I didn't know it then, but I already understood the concept of borrowing authority. I knew that in the end, if people didn't listen to me because of who I was, they still had to respect the authority and the will of the one who sent me. I may not have had the right to ask, but because my father did, what I said had weight, because I went ***in his name***.

When we pray in Jesus' name it is the same way. We are borrowing his authority and His power, because we are going to the Father to do His will. In this way we are like ambassadors in a foreign country. An ambassador is given special rights and privileges because he or she is considered an agent of their king or leader. They do not seek what they want, but what their leader has empowered them to seek. Similarly, praying in Jesus' name means we are using the dominion of Jesus in order to establish the will of Jesus.

Praying in Jesus' name means we are using the dominion of Jesus in order to establish the will of Jesus

These prayers are powerful, first of all, because our own sinfulness and imperfection do not stand in the way. We can be sure that as we approach the father, we have the freedom to ask for more than what we ourselves deserve, because Jesus gives us permission to use His perfection.

The word says that Jesus is the mediator between God and man. When we come to the Father in the name of Jesus, the one who was tempted as we were, yet never fell short, we can approach His throne with boldness.

"Let us therefore come boldly to the throne of grace, that we may obtain mercy and find grace to help in time of need."
Hebrews 4:16 (NKJV)

Equally as important, however, we are only praying in Jesus name if we are sure that what we are praying is something Jesus wants. We can only borrow His authority to do His will. Whenever we pray we must be sure that we are praying for God's will to be established and not our own sinful desires. Sometimes we fail to receive answers to our prayers because our prayers simply went against God's will for us. We are not praying in Jesus name any time we pray for something that would cause us to sin, feed our pride, or pull us away from God. Look at what it says in James 4:2:

"You do not have because you do not ask God. When you ask, you do not receive, because you ask with wrong motives, that you may spend what you get on your pleasures."
James 4:2 (ESV)

Here, the word is describing those who *are* willing to ask God for what they want, but do so with the wrong motive. Asking in Jesus' name means examining your heart, and motives before you pray. God only desires to give us good things, that will be beneficial to us.

If you are praying for something now, examine your heart and seek the truth in the word of God. Ask yourself if your motives are pure, and see what the bible says about what you are asking. If you do not find support for your request in scripture, ask the Lord how you can change your prayer to be a part of His will for your life. Conversely, if you do find support in the word, bring it boldly before the throne of grace. Remember that Jesus said: ***Ask and you will receive, and your joy will be complete.***

Thoughts for Meditation:

Until now, have I asked for my needs in Jesus' name? Or have I been too distracted, afraid, or busy to ask?

Have I leaned on the authority of Jesus when I present my requests to the Father? Or have I tried to ask in my own strength and on my own merit?

Have I asked according to the will of Jesus?

What are some scriptures that support what I have been asking God for?

Prayer:

Dear Heavenly Father, I come before you in Jesus' name. I come before you leaning on His authority, and the power He gave me through the cross. I come before you knowing that it is your will for me to live joyfully, abundant, and complete. Therefore, Lord, I make my requests known to you. I pray that you bring them to completion just as Jesus promised.

(In your own words, complete the prayer by asking God for whatever you need)

9

Come to Me

"Come to me, all you who are weary and burdened, and I will give you rest. Take my yoke upon you and learn from me, for I am gentle and humble in heart, and you will find rest for your souls. For my yoke is easy and my burden is light."
Matthew 11:28-30 (NIV)

In biblical times, the yoke was a long wooden beam that was put on the backs of two animals (usually oxen) so that between the two of them they could pull a heavy cart or carry heavy loads like bags of grain. When Jesus tells us to take His yoke upon us, He's telling us to put down the loads we're carrying that the world gives us (worry, anxiety and stress about all the things we can't control) and instead to take what He has to give us: rest. He is trying to say the only thing He wants us carrying around on our shoulders is joy.

The only thing He wants us carrying around on our shoulders is joy

And that joy will be light and easy for us to bear. Because unlike the world, He is gentle and He doesn't wish for us to be weary or burdened.

What's more, Jesus' reference to the yoke in this passage tells us one other equally important thing: He is holding up the other end of whatever we are going through. Let me explain. When a yoke was used in biblical times each one of the animals carrying it would hold up their end of the beam so that they could share the weight. It was customary at the time to place an older ox or mule with a younger less experienced one. One knew the way, and had done the job many times before. The other could have been scared, confused or inexperienced. But the one who was able, guided the way. Where he had once succeeded, he knew he could succeed again. The inexperienced one had no reason to doubt or be insecure.

> *Although we may be afraid, or wondering if we are going to make it through, He doesn't have to because He has conquered even death itself*

When we take on Jesus' yoke Jesus is holding up the other half of our situation. Although we may be afraid, or wondering if we are going to make it through, He doesn't have to because He has conquered even death itself. He is there to guide us, even when we can't see through the darkness or confusion of a difficult time. Our role is to take His yoke upon us, and simply keep trying.

Sometimes the most difficult part of getting through a season of sadness, is simply not giving up. It can be tempting for us to give up or stop trying. But if we can recognize that Jesus upholds the other half of our situation, and that we aren't required to lead the way, we are liberated from much of the pressure that we may be feeling, and are able to draw strength from Him.

So, we have a choice, we can continue to carry our own yoke and lug around our anxiety, fear and insecurity; or we can decide to learn from Jesus and take on only what He gives us which is much easier to bear. Imagine what could happen if we stopped aiming for perfection and instead chose to seek after Jesus' yoke: joy, love, peace and so much more.

This doesn't mean we can't try to be successful and accomplish our dreams, it just means we don't have to allow the weight that comes with those dreams to lean on our hearts like a heavy yoke. Jesus says it: His yoke is easy; his burden is light.

It's able to be carried without sadness. Learning to share it with Jesus can heal us from the unending weariness caused by a stress-crazed world and we can finally find rest for our souls, and joy in His love.

Thoughts for Meditation:

Have you ever considered the gift that it is to have Jesus walk with you in the midst of troubling times?

How can learning that you do not walk alone increase your joy?

Prayer:

Lord, there are times when I feel so weary and weighed down. I need you to help me, and give me rest for my soul. I'm tired of trying to carry all of my burdens on my own. I'm willing to lay them on you, and receive your yoke, a yoke that is gentle and light.

10

Hope: The Missing Link to Joy

"Rejoice in our confident hope. Be patient in trouble, and keep on praying"
Romans 12:12 (NLT)

Not too long ago I was seeking comfort from the Holy Spirit. I had just returned from the doctor, having just received the news that I had a condition that would make it almost impossible to conceive a child. Although I believed God was going to heal me, I can still remember the emotional sting, the sincere disappointment, and the genuine confusion that I felt as I sat all alone on my dining room table and wept. I remember saying *"Lord, I won't ask you why I have to go through this because that isn't my place, and I won't ask you when you are going to come through because I know that your timing is perfect. The only thing I ask you is HOW. How can I keep on going? Just please show me* ***how*** *I can keep from being swallowed whole by this fear and sadness."*

It was one of the sincerest prayers I've ever prayed as I desperately waited for the Lord to answer. In Proverbs it says that "*hope delayed makes the heart sick,*" and after a very difficult year, my heart was ailing. Just then, I felt the Lord say to my heart, *"trust me and be joyful."*

I slumped down in my chair. It didn't feel like a realistic thing for Him to ask. It seemed like the silly advice someone would give in a movie. I replied, *"Come on, Lord, give me more than that! I know I have to be joyful, but I just don't see anything to be joyful about. Please tell me what to do!"* and I felt the Lord's answer more clearly:

Somewhere along the way my trust was injured.

"You cannot have joy because if you don't trust me. If you trust me you will have hope, and hope is what makes you able to rejoice"

I was stunned. How could I have not seen that my heart was not the only thing that needed mending. Somewhere along the way my trust was injured too. Because I had been disappointed, I subconsciously stopped trusting that the end result of my situation was going to be good. I started to fear that maybe this time it wasn't going to be okay, and God wasn't going to take care of me. I had lost hope.

The word "hope" used in the bible is the word *"elpis,"* a Hebrew word meaning "joyful and confident expectation of what is promised." It's having a positive attitude in troubled times because you believe that there is good ahead. Martin Luther said this when referring to the difference between faith and hope: "They differ in respect of their office, **i.e.** of their working. Faith tells what is to be done, teaches, prescribes, directs; hope stirs up the mind that it may be strong, bold, courageous, that it may suffer and endure adversity, waiting for better things." While faith tells us what to do, hope gives our heart joy so that we do not dismay while we wait. Hope is an attitude that produces a state of joyfulness.

Hope is an attitude that produces a state of joyfulness

This is why in the verse above tells us to rejoice in our confident hope. After all, if we are confident that God is going to do what He said, won't we be joyful? It reminds me of when I was a little girl on Christmas Eve. I was confident that Santa was going to come that night. I was confident that I'd wake up the next day and there would be toys waiting for me under the tree. Santa had never let me down before, so why wouldn't I go to bed with a smile on my face? I remember barely being able to sleep as the joy moved through my bones and made me do a little happy dance right there in bed. Unfortunately, that little girl would eventually grow up, and learn that things don't always go as she hoped, and she would lose that child-like confidence. She would lose trust. She would allow disappointment to blind her so that instead of seeing the wondrous possibilities, when she imagined her future she would only see pain.

So how can we learn to hope again? How can we be joyful even when our world looks as though it's crumbling before us? Look at what the word says a few chapters after the verse we are discussing:

"May the God of hope fill you with all joy and peace as you trust in him, so that you may overflow with hope by the power of the Holy Spirit."
(Romans 15:13 NIV)

Once again, we see that hope and joy are linked. It says here that the God of hope will fill us in joy when we trust in Him. If we want to have joy, we need to re-discover our hope in Jesus. We will need to go back to believing that he WILL do what He said He would do, and that even when we don't understand, His plan is a plan of good towards us.

If we want to have joy, we need to re-discover our hope in Jesus.

Almost all of us know the famous verse Jeremiah 29:11, which says:" *I know the plans I have for you," declares the Lord, "plans to prosper you and not to harm you, plans to give you* **hope** *and a future." (NIV).* However, not all of us live as though Jeremiah 29:11 were a real and unequivocal truth in our lives. In fact, many times with our attitudes we show that our heart doesn't trust it.

We secretly wonder: *Does God really have a plan? Is this part of it? Is it going to harm me? What if I have no hope and no future?*

The truth is, that God does have a plan, and his plan is designed to give us hope! So, we can look toward the future with gladness in our hearts. We can confidently trust that all things—disappointments, trials, and hardships included—are part of a master plan that is good and will be good for us. It is then that we will overflow with hope and find joy again.

The hope of the righteous brings joy, but the expectation of the wicked will perish.
Proverbs 10:2 (NLT)

Thoughts for Meditation:

Have I lost trust in God?

Have I stopped seeing my future with a hopeful attitude?

Have I begun to doubt God's plan for my life?

Has my loss of hope made me sad and downcast? Have I lost my ability to rejoice in confident hope?

Prayer:

Father, please mend my broken heart so that I can trust you again. Help me to look toward my future and confidently expect for you to provide my every need. Although it may not seem like it now, I believe that you are working all things together for my good, as it says in your word. And for that reason, I will choose joy. I will choose to wake up every day with gladness in my heart, expectant of what is to come.

11

Joy vs. Anxiety

"Anxiety in a man's heart weighs him down,
but a good word makes him glad."
Proverbs 12:25 (ESV)

If you've ever experienced anxiety, you know this verse is true. Anxiety is like a weight on the heart. You could be joyful with your faith strong, until an anxious thought creeps in and turns your entire mood around: *What if this all gets taken away? What if it's not what it seems? What is going to happen next?* In an instant you feel weighed down, and sad, even before anything bad happens!

Anxiety is like a weight on the heart

I've experienced this many times. I've been home, relaxing, having a pleasant evening, when someone from work calls to tell me about a problem they've encountered, or complaint they've overheard. If I'm not careful, my pleasant evening can turn into a night of me sulking and asking God why things never go the way I plan. However, what this verse teaches us is that while bad news brings anxiety that weighs us down, a good word has the opposite effect: it makes our heart glad. So, if a good word can combat the effects of anxiety and fear in our hearts, why are we not constantly seeking a good word to make our hearts glad?

A good word is anything that brings encouragement to our hearts. Things that bring us peace and help us to reflect on how thankful we are for what God has done rather than how anxious we are about what hasn't worked out yet. A good word can come from a friend, an uplifting song, and especially from the word of God. The more we fill our hearts with His word, the more His word overpowers the anxiety that weighs us down.

The more we fill our hearts with His word, the more His word overpowers the anxiety that weighs us down

We've all heard the famous cliché: *you are what you eat.* We should treat our hearts the same way. If we feed it gossip, discouragement and fear we will have a heart that is heavy, stressed, and anxious. But when we feed our heart with "*good words*" we become re-energized and joyful.

If anxiety is an issue in your life, I encourage you to fill yourself with good words as much as you can. Read God's word, listen to sermons, and be critical of the music you listen to. Take time to analyze how often you invest in good words for your heart and soul. How often you—possibly unknowingly—let negative words or comments weigh your heart down and fill you with sadness or stress.

Thoughts for Meditation:

How often do you fill your heart with good words?

What are some habits, friendships, or areas in your life that could be inlets for anxiety? How can you close them up or eliminate them from your life?

Make a list of things you can start to do today to get more good words in your system:

Prayer:

Dear God, thank you for the good words that you have placed within my reach. Words that edify me and make my heart glad. Please give me the wisdom to know the difference between those that will do me harm and those that will uplift my heart. Help me to eradicate the anxiety that weighs my heart down and replace it with your everlasting peace.

12

My Father Provides

"Therefore I tell you, do not worry about your life, what you will eat or drink; or about your body, what you will wear. Is not life more than food, and the body more than clothes? Look at the birds of the air; they do not sow or reap or store away in barns, and yet your heavenly Father feeds them. Are you not much more valuable than they? Can any one of you by worrying add a single hour to your life? And why do you worry about clothes? Consider how the flowers in the field grow. They do not labor or spin. Yet I tell you that not even Solomon in all his splendor was dressed like one of these."

Matthew 6:25-29 (NIV)

God loves you and you are valuable to Him. You must believe that in order to break free from fear of the future. As we've already learned: worry is an enemy of joy. What we haven't discussed yet is where worry comes from.

Worry is an enemy of joy

What is it, after all, at the root, that causes us to constantly worry about our future, when Jesus Himself tells us that we don't need to? Perhaps, for one, it's that we don't believe Him.

For many of us, worry stems from insecurity in who we are, and even more importantly: how God feels about us. We worry because at some level we have issues trusting that the creator of all the universe, in fact, taking care of us. It's hard to grasp the idea that the same God that is making sure the earth continues to spin, that all natural processes like flowers growing and birds of the field living, cares for us and values our lives. Whether you believe it or not, the truth is that to God, you are infinitely more important than the birds of the air, and the flowers of the field which He takes meticulous care of every single day.

Understanding the mystery of the love of God doesn't come easy to our human minds

Understanding the mystery of the love of God doesn't come easy to our human minds. I find that often we get too caught up in wanting to know "why." Why he loves us, why we matter, why things are going the way they are.

We often use our questions as a divider between us and God. We are convinced that if we cannot understand it, it must not exist, or is unreliable at best.

In fact, it is such a hard concept to grasp that when the Apostle Paul would pray for the Ephesians he would pray that they would:

> *"...have power, together with all the Lord's holy people, to* ***grasp*** *how wide and long and high and deep is the love of Christ, and to know this love that surpasses knowledge—that you may be filled to the measure of all the fullness of God."*
> *Ephesians 3:18-19 (ESV)*

Note that the word describes God's love as one that surpasses knowledge. Because the first thing that we need to realize is that we will never fully understand the *why*. There is no human measure of logic or intelligence that can explain why a perfect God would love an imperfect person. Paul prayed that the Ephesians would realize this, so that they could learn to accept it, rather than continue trying to understand it. God's love is not something you can memorize, learn or convince yourself of. It is something the Holy Spirit has to reveal to your heart. Only then can you "grasp", as Paul says, the immensity of the love of God. And only then can you begin to live a life free from worry, and truly enjoy living.

When you know that God loves you, you know that He takes special care in even the smallest details of your life. He is up to date on what you need, He knows what you are struggling with. His promise is that He is going to supply your needs on a daily basis, just as he does with the little birds and flowers in the field. Because He loves you, He will not allow harm to befall you and not allow you to be tested beyond your ability. If you trust in this fact, you can live a life as Jesus describes: letting each day worry about itself. After all, worry doesn't help a thing. It doesn't add to our chances of success. It does nothing except rob us of our daily joy.

For a long time, I struggled with the ability to comprehend how deep God's love is for me. I couldn't convince my heart that I was loved; I worried about everything, and constantly feared that I would be a failure or live a life that was insignificant and meaningless.

This continued until I asked the Holy Spirit to reveal to me how loved I am by God. I prayed this prayer every day for some time and sometimes still do when I'm feeling small or afraid. I memorized verses that speak of God's love for me, writing them down and meditating on them day and night. Before long, what was once a doubtful question in my mind as to whether or not God cared, became a deep conviction. When you know God loves you, you can live free of worry and fear. I pray as Paul prayed that we would all come to grasp just how wide and long, and high, and deep, His love is for us.

When you know God loves you, you can live free of worry and fear

Here are some verses about His wonderful love for you to meditate on:

Romans 8:37-39 (ESV)

"...In all these things we are more than conquerors through him who loved us. For I am sure that neither death nor life, nor angels nor rulers, nor things present nor things to come, nor powers, nor height nor depth, nor anything else in all creation, will be able to separate us from the love of God in Christ Jesus our Lord."

1 John 4:16-18 (ESV)

"And so we know and rely on the love God has for us. God is love. Whoever lives in love lives in God, and God in them. This is how love is made complete among us so that we will have confidence on the day of judgment: In this world we are like Jesus. There is no fear in love. But perfect love drives out fear, because fear has to do with punishment. The one who fears is not made perfect in love."

Psalms 103:11(ESV)

"For as high as the heavens are above the earth, so great is his steadfast love toward those who fear him."

Thoughts for Meditation:

How does it feel to know you are deeply loved?

How can confidence in this love cause you to live a life of joy?

What kind of dreams would you dream if you could believe with all your heart that God is taking care of you?What would you dare to accomplish?

Prayer:

Jesus, thank you for treasuring me, loving me, and protecting me. Thank you for clothing me, feeding me, and always taking care of me. Thank you because I don't have to worry about my clothes, or the million things I have to do, because you've told me that you will provide, no matter what the need may be.

13

There Is Wonderful Joy Ahead

"So be truly glad. There is wonderful joy ahead, even though you must endure many trials for a little while. These trials will show that your faith is genuine. It is being tested as fire tests and purifies gold—though your faith is far more precious than mere gold. So when your faith remains strong through many trials, it will bring you much praise and glory and honor on the day when Jesus Christ is revealed to the whole world. You love him even though you have never seen him. Though you do not see him now, you trust him; and you rejoice with a glorious, inexpressible joy."

I Peter 1:6-8 (NLT)

I remember a time in my life where I was enduring many trials. What seems like a lifetime ago, I had what I considered to be the worst year of my life. That was the year that I discovered I had chosen a career path that was not within my gifting and began to feel like a failure because no matter how hard I tried, I couldn't force myself to be passionate about it. Depression snuck into my heart as I healed from painful betrayal in my personal life. Between these two events I was already losing weight and feeling lost. And as if it hadn't been enough, the year ended with my mother's sickness. That year my family struggled, prayed, cried, and finally had to let her go into the arms of her Savior. In such a short time, I felt like I had gone through enough to break me.

That year, I discovered what Peter meant when he said we would endure many trials. However, I also learned that the season of many trials will not last forever. It didn't seem that way in the moment. During those months, hours felt like days, and it seemed as though the tears would never end. But what I did not know or expect is that there was still wonderful joy ahead. During the year of many trials God purified my faith and strengthened my character preparing me to receive new joy.

During the year of many trials, God purified my faith and strengthened my character preparing me to receive new joy

He was making me the kind of person who could truly appreciate, fully utilize, and really understand the joy he was about to give me. Of course, I wish it could have been any other way. No one wants to go through trials. In fact, I'm sure if God had asked me, I might have said, *"No thanks, Lord, leave me where I am. Even though I would like to grow, I don't know if I want to go through the pain!"*

But, fortunately for us, God doesn't give us the choice. Even if we are satisfied with mediocrity, He will keep teaching us until we are purified like gold. He allows temporary trials and tribulations to befall us because He knows in the end, it makes us better and more like Him. As humans, I'm sure we all wish that God's mission were just to make us happy or comfortable. In our earthly mindset we often forget that God is not a genie, he is our father. He is not looking to grant wishes and fill wish lists. He is responsible for training us and making us strong.

I remember being a child and learning my multiplication table. I've never had a head for numbers so it was very difficult for me. My mother, who would help me with my homework, would take extra time quizzing me on my multiplication because she didn't want me to fail the grade. Being young, I would ask her over and over if we could go back to reading and writing, which have always been my great loves. But she would insist we work on math. Now that I'm older, it's obvious to me why: reading and writing were skills I had already developed, I needed to be stretched in the area where I was weak. Hebrews 12:11 sums up this truth perfectly:

Have you ever wondered what area of your capacity is being stretched by your current struggle?

"No discipline seems pleasant at the time, but painful. Later on, however, it produces a harvest of righteousness and peace for those who have been trained by it." (Berean Study Bible)

Have you ever wondered what area of your capacity is being stretched by your current struggle? Perhaps you have asked God to test you in areas where you are already strong, but have received from Him the answer my mom gave me in the second grade: *it's time to learn something new.* My year of pain was definitely not pleasant. At the time it seemed unbearable. However, coming out of a toxic relationship made me free to find a healthy relationship with the man who is now my husband. Switching careers lead me to a Master's in Organizational Behavior which is now one of the centers of my ministry. My mother passing was the single most difficult thing I've had to live through, but it prepared me to inherit her legacy, and made me tough enough to lead a ministry of thousands of people.

In Isaiah 66:9 God promises this to His people, *"I will not cause pain without allowing something new to be born," (NCV)* Before the first edition of this book was published, I remember God brought this verse to life for me in a very real way. I had just experienced my second miscarriage and received the news that my infertility was going to be a longer struggle than I had planned.

That same week, I was scheduled to preach at a conference in California. While I was there, I felt the Lord challenge me to pray for all the women who were having trouble conceiving children. I struggled with this all night. I even asked the Pastor what she wanted me to speak about, hoping she would give me another topic, and an excuse not to have to pray that prayer. Instead, she told me to preach whatever the Lord was putting on my heart. But that would be easier said than done. I felt weak, embarrassed and heartbroken. Part of me didn't want to talk about infertility, much less bring it up in front of hundreds of people, and pray for others when I myself was struggling in that area. Finally, I decided to be obedient to the Holy Spirit. Hundreds of women answered the call and came to the altar for prayer. So I prayed for them.

When I got off the altar, I began to sob. My heart was broken. I too wanted to be a mother. At that moment, one of the speakers, who didn't know me or my situation approached me and said, "The Lord spoke to me and said to tell you that what you have sown in others, you will reap in your own life, you will not only have many children, but God will use you all over the world to break the spirit of infertility." I then realized, what began as nothing more than a painful situation, would be used by God to birth a part of my ministry that I never had before. For months afterwards, I received testimonies of women saying that the Lord had used my prayer to heal them, and that they were pregnant! One woman even conceived quadruplets, and another had triplets! I have learned that pain is only a precursor to joy, if we allow Him, his plan is to use that pain, and cause joy to be born from it. God isn't finished until there is a reason to celebrate.

Though the testing of my faith was painful, it proved to God and myself that my faith is genuine. I learned that to believe in God not just because my parents taught me about Him, or because religion told me to, but because I have a strong enough faith to get through anything, and to provoke God to do miraculous things on my behalf. The verse up above says, "*Though you do not see him now, you trust him; and you rejoice with a glorious, inexpressible joy."* The kind of faith that is produced in these moments of trial produce glorious inexpressible joy when we receive the victory over our circumstances. In fact, James 1:2-4 says this:

"Consider it pure joy, my brothers and sisters, whenever you face trials of many kinds, because you know that the testing of your faith produces perseverance. Let perseverance finish its work so that you may be mature and complete, not lacking anything." (NIV)

Maybe you are lacking joy now, but the word shows us that pure joy comes after trials because it does a work in us that makes us mature and complete. It is only through the fire that we are trained to shine like gold. It is only unpleasant discipline that produces the harvest of peace in our lives. So if today you are enduring hardship, don't give up. There is wonderful joy up ahead.

There is wonderful joy up ahead

Thoughts for Meditation:

What trials are you facing today?

What lessons has God already taught you through these trials?

What kind of wondrous joy are you looking forward to up ahead?

Prayer:

Dear Lord, the trials I am facing are difficult and painful, yet still I will trust you. Help me to find joy as you produce perseverance in me. Help me to look forward to the wondrous joy ahead.

14

Do it for the Joy

"Therefore, since we are surrounded by such a huge crowd of witnesses to the life of faith, let us strip off every weight that slows us down, especially the sin that so easily trips us up. And let us run with endurance the race God has set before us. We do this by keeping our eyes on Jesus, the champion who initiates and perfects our faith. Because of the joy awaiting him, he endured the cross, disregarding its shame. Now he is seated in the place of honor beside God's throne."
Hebrews 12:1-2 (NLT)

It's interesting how the first thing many of us ask when we find ourselves in a difficult situation is *why me*. Many of us have come to mistakenly believe that it is only an unlucky few who have to suffer through hardships. We seem to think that somehow there are people out there living a completely pain-free existence. No trials, no persecutions, just an endless loop of fun and good feels. The truth is actually quite the opposite: we all have a race to run, and we will all have to endure some kind of pain in order to run it.

Even Jesus, the perfect son of God, who witnessed creation and had the power to perform miracles had to endure pain and shame as part of His race. He could have chosen not to. He could have refused. The word of God makes it clear that Jesus had a choice. If He wanted to, He could have circumvented the pain, but He didn't because his focus wasn't the pain; it was the joy set before Him. Jesus understood one very important principle: you can endure any amount of pain if you focus on the prize, rather than the price!

> *We all have a race to run, and we will all have to endure some kind of pain in order to run it*

He knew that at the end of His race, He would be seated in a place of honor at His father's right hand. So, he did what winners do: He endured the pain in order to reap the benefits.

> *You can endure any amount of pain if you focus on the prize, rather than the price!*

Think of anyone you know who has succeeded at something. That person had to make sacrifices and pay a price for their success, regardless of what it was. They understood that in the end, the completion of their goal would make the pain that got them there seem unimportant in comparison.

Jesus' mindset is outlined in Hebrews 12. It was one where He disregarded the shame of the cross. The word disregard means to "pay no attention to; leave out of consideration; or to ignore." Jesus chose not to focus on his pain. Rather than complain about it, avoid it, or fear it, Jesus chose to disregard it. He understood that God has given each of us control over our minds and our thoughts. We chose whether we want to allow our adversities to take over our thinking, and transform our lives, or whether our focus will be the joy that is awaiting us. We need to ask ourselves: What are we setting our minds on? The Bible says in Romans 8:5-6:

> *Jesus chose not to focus on his pain*

"Those who live according to the flesh set their minds on the things of the flesh, but those who live according

to the Spirit set their minds on the things of the Spirit. For to set the mind on the flesh is death, but to set the mind on the Spirit is life and peace." (NIV)

We will never win the race set out for us if our minds are set on the things of the flesh: what our flesh is going through, the pain our flesh feels, the sin and temptations that are pleasurable to our flesh. All of these are earthly things that distract us from what God wants to do in our spirit. Those who chose to concentrate on these things live without because the word says that to set the mind on the flesh is death. However, when we set the mind on the Spirit, we begin to experience life and peace. This is what Jesus did. He chose to ignore the immense suffering He had to endure on a cross.

Can you imagine how much mental discipline this took? Dying on a cross is one of the most gruesome things that a human being could ever endure. It involved nails through your hands, a spear through your side, and eventually hanging naked in front of a crowd as you suffocate to death. Not only was it painful, it was mortifying. Only the worst criminals were sentenced to the cross. Yet, Jesus' mind wasn't set on any of this. His mind was set to the things of the Spirit. While His mind and body were about to be crushed, He knew that His spirit was about to be exalted. He knew that the result of his crucifixion was the next and final level of his race. He was about to finish strong!

He knew that the result of his crucifixion was the next and final level of his race.

"After he has suffered, he will see the light of life and be satisfied; by his knowledge my righteous servant will justify many, and he will bear their iniquities. Therefore, I will give him a portion among the great, and he will divide the spoils with the strong, because he poured out his life unto death,

and was numbered with the transgressors, for he bore the sin of many, and made intercession for the transgressors."
Isaiah 53:11-12 (NIV)

It was Jesus' endurance of great pain that earned him the greatest reward. How different our lives would be if we took this approach to our pain. Sometimes it is so much easier to focus on pain, and forget about the joy that awaits us rather than the other way around. It reminds me of when I gave birth to my son. I was in agony! I remember yelling out, "it feels like my body is attacking me!" and like many other mothers before me, about ten minutes before it was over, I almost gave up. I had labored and toiled, but at the last minute I thought the pain would defeat me. I cried out in suffering, "I don't think I can do it anymore, I just can't." But I remember my husband and cousin saying, "do it for Levi" in other words: *do it for the joy ahead.* With my gaze fixed on my baby, my prize, I was able to withstand the pain of giving birth, and finish strong.

Jesus proved that it is possible to endure the worst possible hardship, yet still be victorious

The word tells us to keep our eyes fixed on Jesus, our champion. The meaning of the word champion is "a person who represents another group of people and brings home a victory for all." Usage of this word began in Ancient Greece to describe an Olympian who earned a victory for his people. It is the one who wins in a competition, and proves that it can be done, and that it can be done well. Jesus proved that it is possible to endure the worst possible hardship, yet still be victorious. He proved that difficult circumstances don't come to us because God hates us, or because we are unlucky, but to teach us how not only to initiate our faith but to complete it.

The word says our champion, Jesus, is the both the initiator and the one who perfects our faith. Another version of this passage says that He is both author and finisher. He began a story with our names in it before we were even born. He set it into motion before the creation of the earth. And day by day He gives us the strength to perfect it, to bring it to a close, to finish it and finish it well. He knows the end before it even begins, and He knows that in the end, if we keep our eyes on Him, we will make it through the pain, to the joy set before us.

Thoughts for Meditation:

What have I set my mind on? Has it been on things of the flesh or on the joy that I know God has set before me?

How can I teach my mind to stay fixed on Jesus?

How can I learn to disregard the painful situations in my life, rather than puff them up or obsess over them?

Prayer:

Jesus, my champion, thank you for enduring the cross and setting the example of a victorious attitude. Today I ask that you put that same mindset in me. Help me to ignore the things of the flesh, and keep my mind on things of the Spirit. Help me to focus on the joy that is coming, rather than the difficulty I must endure, so that like you I can be seated in a place of honor and victory!

Final Thoughts

"The LORD has done great things for us, and we are filled with joy."
Psalm 126:3 (NIV)

We have learned so much already about joy. But, as this book draws to a close, I would like to end on this important note: remember, in everything, to be grateful. Gratitude is an important element in the production of joy in our hearts. When we recognize the greatness of what He has already done for us, two things occur.

For one, we are filled with the joy that stems from simple appreciation for what we have. No, you may not have everything you need, but there was probably a day when you desired what you have now. Let us never forget this truth, and let us never take for granted what we have been given. Let us learn to compare ourselves less to others, and more to who we once were, realizing that we are constantly progressing, and that *that* in itself should bring us joy.

Secondly, gratitude forces us to worship, and worship provokes God to do even more on our behalf. Psalm 69:31-32 says:

"I will praise the name of God with a song; I will magnify him with thanksgiving. This will please the LORD more than an ox or a bull with horns and hoofs. When the humble see it they will be glad; you who seek God, let your

hearts revive. For the LORD hears the needy and does not despise his own people who are prisoners." (ESV)

Sometimes we spend so much time begging God for things that we forget that praise truly touches the heart of the Lord. When our Heavenly Father sees that His children are grateful, He knows He can trust them with more, and causes blessings to rain down on them. Praise is sweeter to Him than a million sacrifices and burnt offerings. Praise moves His fatherly heart.

What's more, as we exalt Him, we become a testimony for others who are going through similar situations. The verse above says "*When the humble see it they will be glad; you who seek God, let your hearts revive.*" We often fail to realize that our reaction to our circumstances does not only affect us: it is seen by everyone around us. If we complain, act like victims, or dwell in self-pity, God cannot be magnified through the situation. It's important to remember what is said in the book of James of our words: they have the power of life and death.

When I was in my single season, I prayed daily for my future husband. After going through two very destructive relationships, I had almost lost hope that God would provide a home and a healthy marriage for me. At one point, after having just gone through a painful break up, I had two friends that were getting married at almost the same time. One of them complained constantly. She complained about her fiancé, the details of the wedding, where she was going to live, and every single thing that happened. I remember being so hurt every time she complained. Here I was desiring a happy relationship, yet she wasn't grateful for hers. Her lack of gratitude discouraged me, making me think maybe I would never be happy.

My other friend, however, was grateful. She rejoiced over everything she had, even if it wasn't the best, newest, or even what she'd planned on. She spoke only positive things about her future husband and his family. This friend gave me hope that "*revived my heart*" as is says it Psalm 69. She was a walking testimony of joy, and I could tell that her grateful attitude not only made her happier, it brightened the lives of the people around her.

Finally, the Psalm above reminds us that the Lord hears the needy. As we lift up gratitude towards Him, He does not forget that we are in need. He knows us better than we know ourselves, and loves us with a love that is almost too deep for comprehension. So, give thanks. Be grateful for even the smallest details in your life, because often those can bring the most joy. Don't withhold your praise because you are going through difficult time. That will only make it more difficult. Instead: choose JOY. Choose to wake up every day and remember the verses we've gone over. Remember that the God who brought you this far will take you the rest of the way.

As this book comes to a close, I can't help but think of how much there is to learn about joy. Reading just one book could never be a complete doctrine, or bring you to an unequivocal understanding of the concept. Joy is a journey. One that I hope you have begun as you've read these pages. I pray that you now see your struggles in a new light. I pray that you are given new hope, and no longer believe that you will die in the land of the dead. And most of all, I pray that through the power of the Holy Spirit, your heart may rejoice in advance for what is to come. Because He who promised is faithful, and there is still wonderful joy ahead.

Acknowledgements

I want to give special thanks to the team that worked so hard to put this book together, make deadlines, and not kill me even with all my craziness and last minute ideas! Thank you for giving your all to make this project a reality, and for complimenting me in all my areas of weakness.

Thank you Sherlyn, who oversaw this project from start to finish and committed to it as though it were her own. To Chris who made my mock-up of the cover come to life. To Mari, my oldest friend and editor. To Maria and Veronica for helping me make this book available in Spanish. To Janessa, for giving your all, and always saving the day. To my father, Pastor Ruddy, for believing in me and giving me the space and freedom to create as a part of my job everyday. And, most of all, to my amazing husband who believes I can do anything and everything, and tells me every day. I am so thankful to have you on my team.

If you liked this book you might also like:

Today, millennials are starting companies, taking control of the media, and conquering the workplace. This generation doesn't only want to be influenced, they want to be influencers. They want to lead, but need to learn how. This book is a highly personal compilation of simple and practical regarding leadership, from the perspective of a young leader. This book will teach you how to begin leading, and how to lay the groundwork for a long and healthy leadership.

"This book is practical yet rich with wisdom. As I read through the pages it was as hearing a sister, a girlfriend, opening up and sharing nuggets of wisdom on what a healthy leader looks like and how I can become one. This book crosses generational lines and is a breath of fresh air to all who are in a position of leadership and influence."
– Ingrid Rosario

"With personal insight, humor, and depth, LEAD provides invaluable direction for leaders of every generation. Vanessa's transparency captures you on every page and will catalyze you into a better you!"
- Lilly Villella Garcia

CPSIA information can be obtained
at www.ICGtesting.com
Printed in the USA
LVHW081023160919
631203LV00017B/316/P

9 781973 662853